HAL·LEONARD
INSTRUMENTAL
PLAY-ALONG

AUDIO
ACCESS
INCLUDED

PLAYBACK+
Speed · Pitch · Balance · Loop

VIOLIN

JAZZ BLUES FAVORITES

Audio arrangements by Peter Deneff

To access audio visit:
www.halleonard.com/mylibrary
Enter Code
6292-2715-7019-5053

ISBN 978-1-4950-5343-6

7777 W. BLUEMOUND RD. P.O. BOX 13819 MILWAUKEE, WI 53213

Visit Hal Leonard Online at
www.halleonard.com

ALL BLUES

Violin

By MILES DAVIS

BASIN STREET BLUES

VIOLIN

Words and Music by
SPENCER WILLIAMS

BIRK'S WORKS

VIOLIN

By DIZZY GILLESPIE

C-JAM BLUES

VIOLIN

By DUKE ELLINGTON

FREDDIE FREELOADER

Violin

By MILES DAVIS

MR. P.C.

VIOLIN

By JOHN COLTRANE

NIGHT TRAIN

VIOLIN

Words by OSCAR WASHINGTON
and LEWIS C. SIMPKINS
Music by JIMMY FORREST

NOW'S THE TIME

Violin

By CHARLIE PARKER

ONE FOR DADDY-O

Violin

By NAT ADDERLY

THE SWINGIN' SHEPHERD BLUES

VIOLIN

Words and Music by MOE KOFFMAN,
RHODA ROBERTS and KENNY JACOBSON

TENOR MADNESS

VIOLIN

By SONNY ROLLINS

THINGS AIN'T WHAT THEY USED TO BE

Violin

By MERCER ELLINGTON

Hal•Leonard INSTRUMENTAL PLAY-ALONG

Your favorite songs are arranged just for solo instrumentalists with this outstanding series. Each book includes a great full-accompaniment play-along audio so you can sound just like a pro! Check out www.halleonard.com to see all the titles available.

Chart Hits

All About That Bass • All of Me • Happy • Radioactive • Roar • Say Something • Shake It Off • A Sky Full of Stars • Someone like You • Stay with Me • Thinking Out Loud • Uptown Funk.

____	00146207	Flute	$12.99
____	00146208	Clarinet	$12.99
____	00146209	Alto Sax	$12.99
____	00146210	Tenor Sax	$12.99
____	00146211	Trumpet	$12.99
____	00146212	Horn	$12.99
____	00146213	Trombone	$12.99
____	00146214	Violin	$12.99
____	00146215	Viola	$12.99
____	00146216	Cello	$12.99

Coldplay

Clocks • Every Teardrop Is a Waterfall • Fix You • In My Place • Lost! • Paradise • The Scientist • Speed of Sound • Trouble • Violet Hill • Viva La Vida • Yellow.

____	00103337	Flute	$12.99
____	00103338	Clarinet	$12.99
____	00103339	Alto Sax	$12.99
____	00103340	Tenor Sax	$12.99
____	00103341	Trumpet	$12.99
____	00103342	Horn	$12.99
____	00103343	Trombone	$12.99
____	00103344	Violin	$12.99
____	00103345	Viola	$12.99
____	00103346	Cello	$12.99

Disney Greats

Arabian Nights • Hawaiian Roller Coaster Ride • It's a Small World • Look Through My Eyes • Yo Ho (A Pirate's Life for Me) • and more.

____	00841934	Flute	$12.99
____	00841935	Clarinet	$12.99
____	00841936	Alto Sax	$12.99
____	00841937	Tenor Sax	$12.95
____	00841938	Trumpet	$12.99
____	00841939	Horn	$12.95
____	00841940	Trombone	$12.95
____	00841941	Violin	$12.99
____	00841942	Viola	$12.95
____	00841943	Cello	$12.99
____	00842078	Oboe	$12.99

Great Themes

Bella's Lullaby • Chariots of Fire • Get Smart • Hawaii Five-O Theme • I Love Lucy • The Odd Couple • Spanish Flea • and more.

____	00842468	Flute	$12.99
____	00842469	Clarinet	$12.99
____	00842470	Alto Sax	$12.99
____	00842471	Tenor Sax	$12.99
____	00842472	Trumpet	$12.99
____	00842473	Horn	$12.99
____	00842474	Trombone	$12.99
____	00842475	Violin	$12.99
____	00842476	Viola	$12.99
____	00842477	Cello	$12.99

Lennon & McCartney Favorites

All You Need Is Love • A Hard Day's Night • Here, There and Everywhere • Hey Jude • Let It Be • Nowhere Man • Penny Lane • She Loves You • When I'm Sixty-Four • and more.

____	00842600	Flute	$12.99
____	00842601	Clarinet	$12.99
____	00842603	Tenor Sax	$12.99
____	00842604	Trumpet	$12.99
____	00842605	Horn	$12.99
____	00842607	Violin	$12.99
____	00842608	Viola	$12.99
____	00842609	Cello	$12.99

Popular Hits

Breakeven • Fireflies • Halo • Hey, Soul Sister • I Gotta Feeling • I'm Yours • Need You Now • Poker Face • Viva La Vida • You Belong with Me • and more.

____	00842511	Flute	$12.99
____	00842512	Clarinet	$12.99
____	00842513	Alto Sax	$12.99
____	00842514	Tenor Sax	$12.99
____	00842515	Trumpet	$12.99
____	00842516	Horn	$12.99
____	00842517	Trombone	$12.99
____	00842518	Violin	$12.99
____	00842519	Viola	$12.99
____	00842520	Cello	$12.99

Songs from Frozen, Tangled and Enchanted

Do You Want to Build a Snowman? • For the First Time in Forever • Happy Working Song • I See the Light • In Summer • Let It Go • Mother Knows Best • That's How You Know • True Love's First Kiss • When Will My Life Begin • and more.

____	00126921	Flute	$14.99
____	00126922	Clarinet	$14.99
____	00126923	Alto Sax	$14.99
____	00126924	Tenor Sax	$14.99
____	00126925	Trumpet	$14.99
____	00126926	Horn	$14.99
____	00126927	Trombone	$14.99
____	00126928	Violin	$14.99
____	00126929	Viola	$14.99
____	00126930	Cello	$14.99

Top Hits

Adventure of a Lifetime • Budapest • Die a Happy Man • Ex's & Oh's • Fight Song • Hello • Let It Go • Love Yourself • One Call Away • Pillowtalk • Stitches • Writing's on the Wall.

____	00171073	Flute	$12.99
____	00171074	Clarinet	$12.99
____	00171075	Alto Sax	$12.99
____	00171106	Tenor Sax	$12.99
____	00171107	Trumpet	$12.99
____	00171108	Horn	$12.99
____	00171109	Trombone	$12.99
____	00171110	Violin	$12.99
____	00171111	Viola	$12.99
____	00171112	Cello	$12.99

Wicked

As Long As You're Mine • Dancing Through Life • Defying Gravity • For Good • I'm Not That Girl • Popular • The Wizard and I • and more.

____	00842236	Flute	$12.99
____	00842237	Clarinet	$11.99
____	00842238	Alto Saxophone	$11.95
____	00842239	Tenor Saxophone	$11.95
____	00842240	Trumpet	$11.99
____	00842241	Horn	$11.95
____	00842242	Trombone	$12.99
____	00842243	Violin	$11.99
____	00842244	Viola	$12.99
____	00842245	Cello	$12.99

HAL•LEONARD®

101 SONGS

YOUR FAVORITE SONGS ARE ARRANGED FOR
SOLO INSTRUMENTALISTS WITH THIS GREAT SERIES.

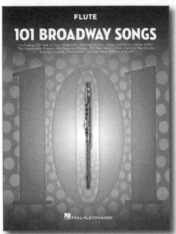

101 BROADWAY SONGS

Cabaret • Do You Hear the People Sing? • Edelweiss • Guys and Dolls • Hello, Dolly! • I Dreamed a Dream • If I Were a Bell • Luck Be a Lady • Ol' Man River • Seasons of Love • Send in the Clowns • Think of Me • Tomorrow • What I Did for Love • and many more.

00154199	Flute		$14.99
00154200	Clarinet		$14.99
00154201	Alto Sax		$14.99
00154202	Tenor Sax		$14.99
00154203	Trumpet		$14.99
00154204	Horn		$14.99
00154205	Trombone		$14.99
00154206	Violin		$14.99
00154207	Viola		$14.99
00154208	Cello		$14.99

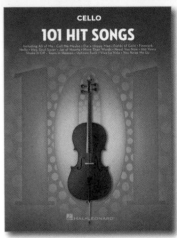

101 HIT SONGS

All About That Bass • All of Me • Brave • Breakaway • Clocks • Fields of Gold • Firework • Hey, Soul Sister • Ho Hey • I Gotta Feeling • Jar of Hearts • Love Story • 100 Years • Roar • Rolling in the Deep • Shake It Off • Smells like Teen Spirit • Uptown Funk • and more.

00194561	Flute		$16.99
00197182	Clarinet		$16.99
00197183	Alto Sax		$16.99
00197184	Tenor Sax		$16.99
00197185	Trumpet		$16.99
00197186	Horn		$16.99
00197187	Trombone		$16.99
00197188	Violin		$16.99
00197189	Viola		$16.99
00197190	Cello		$16.99

101 CLASSICAL THEMES

Ave Maria • Bist du bei mir (You Are with Me) • Canon in D • Clair de Lune • Dance of the Sugar Plum Fairy • 1812 Overture • Eine Kleine Nachtmusik ("Serenade"), First Movement Excerpt • The Flight of the Bumble Bee • Funeral March of a Marionette • Fur Elise • Gymnopedie No. 1 • Jesu, Joy of Man's Desiring • Lullaby • Minuet in G • Ode to Joy • Piano Sonata in C • Pie Jesu • Rondeau • Theme from Swan Lake • Wedding March • William Tell Overture • and many more.

00155315	Flute		$14.99
00155317	Clarinet		$14.99
00155318	Alto Sax		$14.99
00155319	Tenor Sax		$14.99
00155320	Trumpet		$14.99
00155321	Horn		$14.99
00155322	Trombone		$14.99
00155323	Violin		$14.99
00155324	Viola		$14.99
00155325	Cello		$14.99

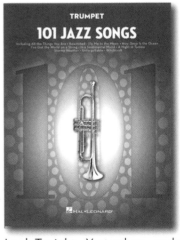

101 JAZZ SONGS

All of Me • Autumn Leaves • Bewitched • Blue Skies • Body and Soul • Cheek to Cheek • Come Rain or Come Shine • Don't Get Around Much Anymore • A Fine Romance • Here's to Life • I Could Write a Book • It Could Happen to You • The Lady Is a Tramp • Like Someone in Love • Lullaby of Birdland • The Nearness of You • On Green Dolphin Street • Satin Doll • Stella by Starlight • Tangerine • Unforgettable • The Way You Look Tonight • Yesterdays • and many more.

00146363	Flute		$14.99
00146364	Clarinet		$14.99
00146366	Alto Sax		$14.99
00146367	Tenor Sax		$14.99
00146368	Trumpet		$14.99
00146369	Horn		$14.99
00146370	Trombone		$14.99
00146371	Violin		$14.99
00146372	Viola		$14.99
00146373	Cello		$14.99

www.halleonard.com

Prices, contents and availability subject to change without notice.

O217